NEW!

# The DISCOVERY HAGGADAH


by

Rabbi Kerry M. Olitzky

Rabbi Ronald H. Isaacs

illustrated by Arthur Friedman



…G HOUSE, INC

For the memory of Bubbe's gefilte fish
and Zeyde's horseradish
at Pesach,
whose taste
continues to liberate us.



ISBN 0-88125-987-X
Printed in USA

## TABLE OF CONTENTS

Thanks to Deborah Hercky for the rap on page 32.

## A Note for Parents and Teachers

This Haggadah leads you on a discovery to find the Pesach Seder that is most meaningful for your students or family. The essential Seder service is contained in this Haggadah and is written in a voice easily understood by growing-up families and children. Each section and subsection is introduced by "why," which explains the reason behind the specific section, and "how to," which gives simple, direct instruction for completing that part of the Seder. The traditional text with explanation is included. The activities for discovery follow. Try them out and add your own. They are particularly good for model *Sedarim* in schools. But be careful. Don't try to do them all at once. Leave some for your *Sedarim* in years to come.

Here is the key:

Questions

Innovations

Imagination

New Songs

Games to Play

Curiosities

The beauty of the Haggadah is that it contains the hopes and aspirations—and even the fears—of each generation. It is truly a sacred living text. We pray that the Haggadah is part of the fabric of your family and students as it is of our own.

Yom Ha-atzmaut, 5751

Rabbi Kerry M. Olitzky
Rabbi Ronald H. Isaacs

## Seder Symbols

זְרוֹעַ

*Zeroa:* Symbol of the Pesach offering; usually a roasted shankbone (or a boiled beet for vegetarians).

כַּרְפַּס

*Karpas:* Symbol of spring; a green vegetable, usually parsley.

מָרוֹר

*Maror:* Symbol of the bitterness of slave life; bitter herbs, usually horseradish.

מַצּוֹת

*Matzot:* Symbol of slavery, poverty, and the Exodus; three pieces covered.

בֵּיצָה

*Betzah:* Symbol of the festival offering; a roasted egg (or an avocado seed for vegetarians).

חֲזֶרֶת

*Chazeret:* Optional on some Seder plates; an additional variety of bitter herbs to be used for the korech sandwich (usually romaine lettuce).

חֲרֹסֶת

*Charoset:* Symbol of mortar; a mixture, usually of chopped apples, chopped nuts, wine, and spices.

# בְּדִיקַת חָמֵץ

## Bedikat Chametz

## Getting Ready for the Seder

*Bedikat Chametz:* After you have done your Pesach spring cleaning, collect all the remaining chametz in your home the night before Pesach. Search it out with candle, feather, and spoon. Set a small amount aside until morning, when we symbolically burn it (*biur chametz*). Recite the text from Exodus with the blessing before the search. After the chametz has been removed, recite the second blessing.

"Remember this day as the day you left Egypt, from the house of slavery. It was with a mighty hand that Adonai led you out. No chametz should be eaten" (Exodus 13:3).

זָכוֹר אֶת־הַיּוֹם הַזֶּה אֲשֶׁר
יְצָאתֶם מִמִּצְרַיִם מִבֵּית עֲבָדִים
כִּי בְּחֹזֶק יָד הוֹצִיא יְיָ אֶתְכֶם
מִזֶּה וְלֹא יֵאָכֵל חָמֵץ:

Praised are You, Adonai our God, Guide of the Universe, who gave us the special gift of mitzvot and instructed us to remove chametz from our homes.

בָּרוּךְ אַתָּה יְיָ, אֱלֹהֵינוּ מֶלֶךְ
הָעוֹלָם, אֲשֶׁר קִדְּשָׁנוּ
בְּמִצְוֹתָיו, וְצִוָּנוּ עַל־בִּעוּר
חָמֵץ:

**Ba-ruch a-tah A-do-nai E-lo-hey-nu me-lech ha-o-lam, a-sher kid-sha-nu b'-mitz-vo-tav v'tzi-va-nu al bi-ur cha-metz**

I am ready to welcome the Festival of Matzot into our home. May it bring us close to freedom and peace.

*Maot Chittim:* Tzedakah called "wheat money" is collected to help buy Passover foods for the poor. You may even want to donate your chametz to non-Jews who are hungry.

## The Seder (Order) of The Seder

The Seder program consists of fourteen different ceremonies. To make it easier to remember, the ceremonial names are sung to a special melody . . . Kadesh, Urchatz . . .

1. קַדֵּשׁ

1. KADESH: Special and Holy

2. וּרְחַץ

2. URCHATZ: Washing

3. כַּרְפַּס

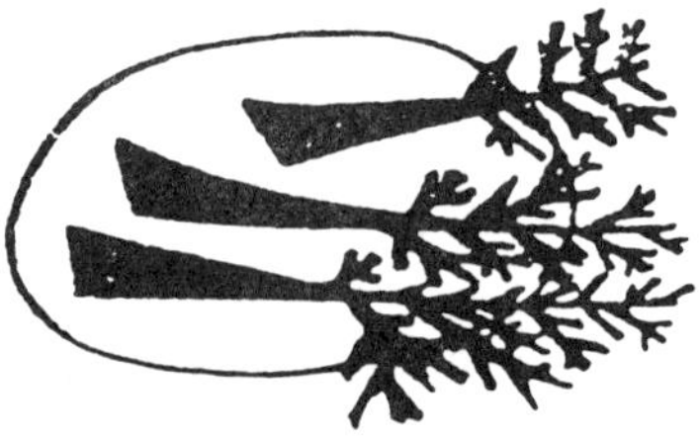

3. KARPAS: Green Things

4. יַחַץ

4. YACHATZ: Break It in the Middle

5. מַגִּיד

5. MAGID: The Telling and Retelling

6. רָחְצָה

6. RACHTZAH: Cleansing

7. מוֹצִיא מַצָּה

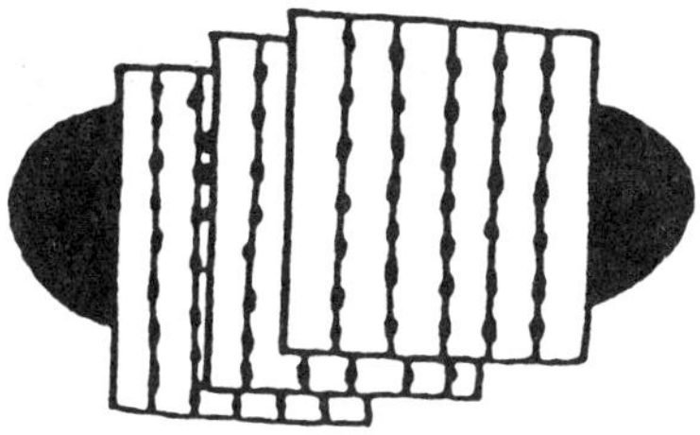

7. MOTZI MATZAH:
Eating Matzah "Bread"

8. מָרוֹר

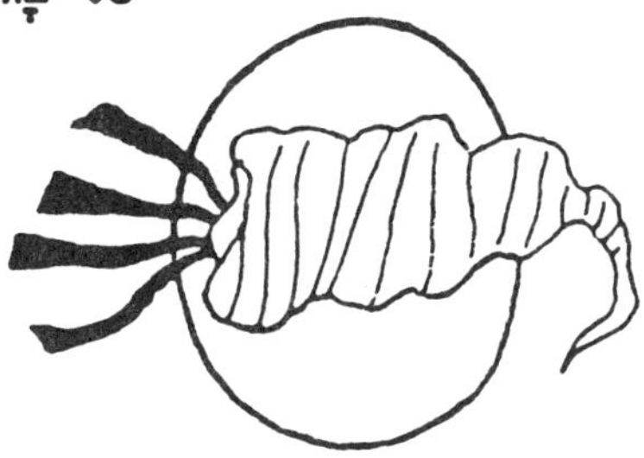

8. MAROR: Bitter Horseradish

9. כּוֹרֵךְ

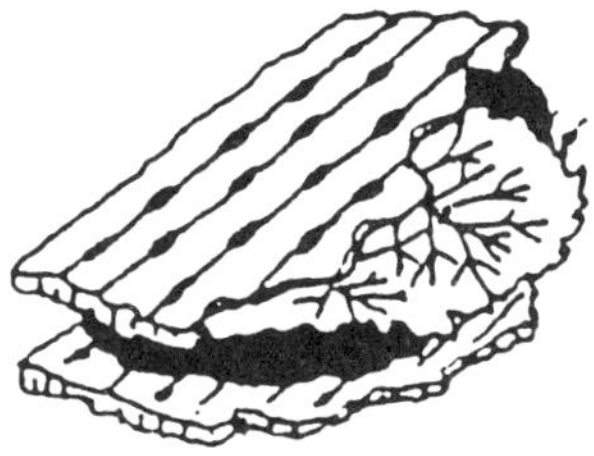

9. KORECH: Hillel's Sandwich

10. שֻׁלְחָן עוֹרֵךְ

10. SHULCHAN ORECH:
The Meal Is Served

11. צָפוּן

11. TZAFUN:
The Hidden Afikoman

12. בָּרֵךְ

12. BARECH: Giving Thanks

13. הַלֵּל

13. HALLEL: Songs of Praise

14. נִרְצָה

14. NIRTZAH: Acceptance

## Are You Ready?

Holiday candles
Pesach wine
Seder plate
Elijah's Cup
Three pieces of matzah with cover
Pillow for getting comfortable
Salt water
Cup, bowl, and towel for ritual washing
Haggadot (one for each person)
Wine cups (one for each person)

Extras:
Flowers
Freedom clothes (traditionally a white kittel)
An extra wine cup of freedom
An extra place-setting for oppressed Jewish families who cannot freely celebrate
An extra matzah (of hope)

# THE SEDER

# קַדֵּשׁ

## Kadesh: Special and Holy

**WHY:** Just as on every festival and every Shabbat, we mark the specialness of the day by saying a special blessing over a cup of wine. The Kiddush is particularly important on Pesach because each time we say it we are reminded of *yitziyat Mitzrayim*—the Exodus from Egypt. On our way to Canaan (now called Israel), we received the Torah and slowly but surely became the Jewish people. We drink four cups during the Seder, one for each promise God made to our Israelite ancestors in Egypt. This one is for "I will free you from the burden of [working as a slave for] the Egyptians" (Exod. 6:6).

**HOW TO:** Fill your glass with wine (or grape juice). You'll have to do this four times during the Seder. It's OK to fill it full and let it spill over a little, since our hearts are filled up with happiness about leaving slavery behind in Egypt. Drink the wine *after* you have said the whole blessing. And don't forget to get comfortable. Special table manners tonight. You're *free* to sit in a way that's most comfortable for you.

### A Place for Seder Thoughts of My Own

Start here

# כּוֹס רִאשׁוֹנָה

## Kos Rishohnah
## The First Cup

Heneni muchan u'mizuman. I am ready to fulfill the mitzvah of drinking the first cup of wine.

הִנְנִי מוּכָן וּמְזֻמָּן לְקַיֵּם מִצְוַת כּוֹס רִאשׁוֹנָה

Praised are You, Adonai our God, Guide of the Universe, who creates fruit that grows on the vine.

בָּרוּךְ אַתָּה יְיָ, אֱלֹהֵינוּ מֶלֶךְ הָעוֹלָם, בּוֹרֵא, פְּרִי הַגָּפֶן:

**Ba-ruch a-tah A-do-nai, E-lo-hey-nu me-lech ha-o-lam, bo-rey p'-ri ha-ga-fen.**

Praised are You, Adonai our God, Guide of the Universe, who chose us from among the peoples by giving us the special gift of mitzvot. Out of love, You have given us happy holidays to celebrate, including this terrific Pesach, our time of freedom, a special and holy time to help us remember *yitziyat Mitzrayim*—the Exodus from Egypt. You have chosen us, separating us from other peoples by special festivals which we happily celebrate. Praised are You, Adonai, who makes special and holy the people of Israel and its festivals.

בָּרוּךְ אַתָּה יְיָ, אֱלֹהֵינוּ מֶלֶךְ הָעוֹלָם, אֲשֶׁר בָּחַר בָּנוּ מִכָּל-עָם, וְרוֹמְמָנוּ מִכָּל-לָשׁוֹן, וְקִדְּשָׁנוּ בְּמִצְוֹתָיו, וַתִּתֶּן לָנוּ יְיָ אֱלֹהֵינוּ בְּאַהֲבָה מוֹעֲדִים לְשִׂמְחָה, חַגִּים וּזְמַנִּים לְשָׂשׂוֹן, אֶת־יוֹם חַג הַמַּצּוֹת הַזֶּה. זְמַן חֵרוּתֵנוּ, מִקְרָא קֹדֶשׁ, זֵכֶר לִיצִיאַת מִצְרָיִם. כִּי בָנוּ בָחַרְתָּ, וְאוֹתָנוּ קִדַּשְׁתָּ, מִכָּל-הָעַמִּים. וּמוֹעֲדֵי קָדְשֶׁךָ בְּשִׂמְחָה וּבְשָׂשׂוֹן הִנְחַלְתָּנוּ: בָּרוּךְ אַתָּה יְיָ, מְקַדֵּשׁ יִשְׂרָאֵל וְהַזְּמַנִּים:

drink first cup of "wine"

*Kiddush, kadesh*, and *kadosh* all come from the Hebrew word meaning "holy" or "special." What does the word "holy" mean to you? Talk about some times when you felt holy. Describe an object in your home which you think is holy.

The first line of the Kiddush describes God choosing us to be special people. In what way do you feel special? Talk about a time when someone chose you to do something special.

Why do we recline on the left side?

The name "Pesach" probably comes from the Hebrew word *pasach*, meaning "to pass over." Ask everyone at your Seder, in turn, to tell the group about something they would not want to pass over.

Here are some things that we cannot "pass over" on Pesach:

a. Concern for those who are not free
b. Remembering our loved ones
c. Concern for the environment
d. Feeding the hungry

Set aside an extra cup of wine (in addition to the one already prepared for Elijah the Prophet). Leave this cup empty. Tell everyone at the Seder that this cup is to honor all those who are not free to join your Passover Seder.

Go outside and look at the full moon. Why does Passover begin with a full moon?

Reserve an extra chair and complete place-setting for all Jews who are still "slaves." Place a pillow on it as a symbol of hope for a time when they will be at ease.

German Jews often use white wine instead of red so that it is not mistaken for blood.

In the past, Jews began their Sedarim by opening the door and inviting all who were hungry to come and eat. As persecutions of the Jews increased, such announcements became dangerous and the "open door" policy was used to make sure no one was at the door listening.

Yemenite Jews sprinkle their clothing with incense before the Seder to make the night even more special. And Jews from the Caucasus Mountains in the southern part of the Soviet Union used to wear loose-fitting tunic-like garments which they called "liberty clothes."

## A Place for Seder Thoughts of My Own

# וּרְחַץ

## Urchatz: Washing

**WHY:** Since the Seder is so special, we make a big deal out of washing our hands and getting ready. We want to make them ritually clean because we are going to do holy things.

**HOW TO:** Use a pitcher or cup and pour water over each hand, one at a time. No need to say the blessing for washing hands yet. We'll save that for later.

Why do you think we wash our hands without a blessing?

Look at the letters in this Passover Word Game. What Passover words can you find? Give yourself one point for each correct answer. See who can find the most words most quickly at the Seder.

| | | | | | |
|---|---|---|---|---|---|
| M | V | K | E | N | I |
| A | S | I | G | P | O |
| T | T | D | Y | R | M |
| Z | J | L | P | B | E |
| A | W | A | T | E | R |
| H | B | S | A | L | T |

Some say that we wash our hands because in ancient times it was a custom to do so before dipping things in liquids. Liquids were considered to pass on ritual impurity. Others say we do so because the ancient priests washed before approaching the Temple altar. Tonight, the table is transformed into a sacred altar.

The answers are on p. 79.

# כַּרְפַּס

## Karpas: Green Things

**WHY:** Spring is a special time of year. Everything seems to come alive again after being dormant all winter—even if you live in Florida or California. It is also the rebirth of the Jewish people. But all was not perfect. There were lots of salty tears when we were slaves. That's why we dip greens into salt water—to mix our sadness with the hope that spring brings to life.

**HOW TO:** Take your green vegetable, usually parsley, and dip it in salt water. (This is your first dipping; remember that when you ask the Four Questions.) Then eat it, but say the blessing first. Yes, you can slouch for this one too.

Praised are You, Adonai our God, Guide of the Universe, who creates things that grow in the ground.

בָּרוּךְ אַתָּה יְיָ, אֱלֹהֵינוּ מֶלֶךְ
הָעוֹלָם, בּוֹרֵא, פְּרִי הָאֲדָמָה:

**Ba-ruch a-tah A-do-nai, E-lo-hey-nu me-lech ha-o-lam, bo-rey p'ri ha-a-da-mah.**

Serve platefuls of karpas appetizer (celery, carrots, parsley, radishes) along with some dip so that those who are really hungry can come and eat something before the meal.

Again chant the *seder* ("order") of the Seder. But this time, stop at the step in the Seder just about to be celebrated. For example, when you reach the karpas part of the Seder, before actually doing the karpas ritual, chant up to "Karpas." This is like an announcement for the next step in the Seder. Continue this rechanting of the steps each time you come to a new section throughout the Seder.

Rabbi Yehudah said: "Someone who goes out in the month of Nisan and sees the trees in bloom should recite the blessing: 'Praised are You, Adonai, who has not left the world lacking in anything and has created in it good trees to give pleasure to humankind' " (Babylonian Talmud, Berachot 43b). Go outside, find a new spring blossom, and recite this blessing!

People wonder whether any type of green vegetable can be used for karpas. The *Code of Jewish Law* suggests that we use parsley but also strongly encourages us to eat celery and even radishes (118:2).

Greeks and Romans would often dip hors d'oeuvres before they ate a big banquet meal!

# יַחַץ

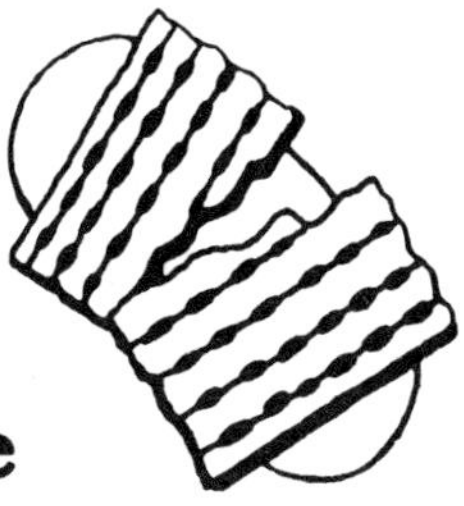

## Yachatz: Break it in the Middle

**WHY:** There are lots of reasons why we stack three pieces of matzah and then break the middle one. Since we use two loaves of challah for Shabbat and festivals (one loaf representing the ordinary bread of every day and the extra one for the extra pre-Shabbat portion of heavenly manna), we add a third to remind us that matzah is the *bread* of affliction. The three pieces also remind us that as Jews we are all in this together whether our ancestors were *Kohanim* (priests), Levites (assistant priests), or Israelites (just plain folks). We break bread—the middle matzah—to be hospitable to everyone we have invited to share the Seder with us. We also do it to emphasize how little we had to eat as slaves, but in an unusual sort of way this shared matzah experience binds us all together as a people.

The afikoman is wrapped up in much the same way as the Israelites wrapped their baking tools when they quickly left Egypt.

**HOW TO:** Take the three pieces of matzah you have set aside for the Seder. Break the middle matzah into two pieces. ~~Let someone hide one of the broken pieces as the afikoman. Don't look! We'll search for it later.~~ Then put back the other broken piece between the two unbroken pieces.

In some European families, when the leader is not looking, the children hide the afikoman and ransom it later.

Yemenite tradition suggests that the name "afikoman" came from these words:

| | |
|---|---|
| אגוזים | nuts |
| פרות | fruit |
| יין | wine |
| קליות | roasted things |
| ובשר | and meat |
| מים | water |
| נרד | spikenard |

Moroccan Jews have a tradition of tossing the afikoman into the sea (prior to a voyage) in order to calm the seas and prevent storms (from Psalm 54:9 : “God has saved me from all trouble ”).

If you could invite anyone to your Seder to join you in this meal, who would you invite? Why?

Add one more matzah to the pile. Call it a matzah of hope. Lift it and set it aside as a symbol for all Jews throughout the world who are still not free enough to celebrate a Passover Seder. You may also want to talk a little about what your family might be able to do to help them gain their freedom.

Sephardic Jews place the wrapped afikoman in a bag, which is then thrown over the shoulder and carried around the Seder table. This makes us feel like we are rushing out of Egypt like our ancestors did during the Exodus.

Jewish mystics (known as Kabbalists) break the middle matzah into the shape of the Hebrew letters *daled* and *vav,* the fourth and sixth letters of the alphabet. According to gematria, this makes a total of 10, equaling the number of *sefirot,* or levels of mystical spheres, in the universe. See if you can do it.

In some communities there used to be a custom of inscribing the three matzot with the words Kohen, Levi, and Israelite. Other communities marked them with the first three letters of the Hebrew alphabet.

# מַגִּיד

## Magid: The Telling and Retelling

**WHY:** This begins the retelling of the story of how the Israelites were slaves in Egypt and eventually were freed by God under the leadership of Moses. The whole saga is symbolized by the matzah. When we look at it, we try to remember what it was like to have been slaves in Egypt, because in a funny sort of way, we were all there. We invite others to share in the Seder meal and to hear the story of our ancestors. We remember what it was like to be strangers in a strange land, and so we invite guests to our table. We begin with Ha Lachma Anya because not all of our people are free even today. Some are still forced to live like slaves.

**HOW TO:** Uncover the matzah. Hold it up so that all can see it and then read the Ha Lachma Anya. You may want to add your own prayer at this point in the Seder for those of our brothers and sisters who are still struggling to breathe free.

הָא לַחְמָא עַנְיָא, דִּי אֲכָלוּ אַבְהָתָנָא בְּאַרְעָא דְמִצְרָיִם. כָּל-דִּכְפִין יֵיתֵי וְיֵכֻל, כָּל-דִּצְרִיךְ יֵיתֵי וְיִפְסַח. הָשַּׁתָּא הָכָא, לְשָׁנָה הַבָּאָה בְּאַרְעָא דְיִשְׂרָאֵל. הָשַּׁתָּא עַבְדֵי, לְשָׁנָה הַבָּאָה בְּנֵי חוֹרִין:

Ha Lachma Anya: This is the Bread of Poverty which our ancestors ate in the land of Egypt. Let all who are hungry come join us for the meal. Let all who are in need come and celebrate Pesach with us. Now we are here. May we be in the land of Israel next year. Now we are slaves. May we all be free next year.

Remove the Seder plate or place it at the end of the table. This will help to stimulate everyone's curiosity. It can later be moved back to the center of the table.

Among Moroccan families, the middle matzah is broken into two pieces to resemble the Hebrew letter *hay,* standing for God. At the same time, everyone sings an Arabic song which recalls the miracle of the Red Sea. This *hay*-shaped matzah is then taken by each member of the family and held against their eyes as the Ha Lahma Anya is recited.

Bukharan Jews stand up during the Magid section and walk around the Seder table in a bent-over posture, as if they were still slaves.

# מַה נִּשְׁתַּנָּה

## Mah Nishtanah?
## One Big Question:
## Four Big Answers

**WHY:** Since the Magid section of the Seder is the retelling of the Pesach story, it is natural to begin with an answer to the question: Why Pesach? The Four Questions really started as examples of questions that might be asked to begin the Seder, but they quickly became favorites. And now everyone asks the same questions in pretty much the same way. The big question remains: Why *is* this night of the Seder so different from all other nights?

**HOW TO:** Anyone can ask the questions, but usually the youngest person at the Seder reads the Mah Nishtanah. Read or sing or chant them one at a time, then take a deep breath and relax. Listen to the answers for a couple of hours. But re-cover the matzah and fill your cup a second time. You will want to get ready for what comes next.

## מַה נִּשְׁתַּנָּה הַלַּיְלָה הַזֶּה, מִכָּל-הַלֵּילוֹת?

How different is this night of Seder from all other nights!

**Ma nish-ta-nah ha-lai-lah ha-zeh mi-kol ha-ley-lot!**

1) שֶׁבְּכָל הַלֵּילוֹת, אָנוּ אוֹכְלִין חָמֵץ וּמַצָּה, הַלַּיְלָה הַזֶּה כֻּלּוֹ מַצָּה:

On all other nights, we eat either chametz or matzah.
Why do we only eat matzah tonight?

**1) She-b'-chol he-ley-lot a-nu och-lin cha-meytz u-ma-tzah, ha-lai-lah ha-zeh ku-lo-ma-tzah.**

2) שֶׁבְּכָל הַלֵּילוֹת אָנוּ אוֹכְלִין שְׁאָר יְרָקוֹת, הַלַּיְלָה הַזֶּה מָרוֹר:

On all other nights we (try to) eat all kinds of vegetables.
Why do we only eat bitter horseradish tonight?

**2) She-b'-chol ha-ley-lot a-nu och-lin sh'-ar y'-ra-kot, ha-lai-lah ha-zeh ma-ror.**

3) שֶׁבְּכָל הַלֵּילוֹת אֵין אָנוּ מַטְבִּילִין, אֲפִילוּ פַּעַם אֶחָת, הַלַּיְלָה הַזֶּה שְׁתֵּי פְעָמִים:

On all other nights we usually don't dip our vegetables at all.
Why do we dip our vegetables twice tonight?

**3) She-b'-chol ha-ley-lot eyn a-nu mat-bi-lin a-fi-lu pa-am e-chat, ha-lai-la ha-zeh sh'-tey f'-a-mim.**

4) שֶׁבְּכָל הַלֵּילוֹת, אָנוּ אוֹכְלִין, בֵּין יוֹשְׁבִין, וּבֵין מְסֻבִּין, הַלַּיְלָה הַזֶּה כֻּלָּנוּ מְסֻבִּין:

On all other nights we eat either sitting straight or sitting in a relaxed position.
Why do we eat sitting only in a relaxed position tonight?

**4) She-b'-chol ha-ley-lot a-nu och-lin beyn yosh-vin u-veyn m'-su-bin, ha-lai-la ha-zeh ku-la-nu m'-su-bin.**

What are some other questions that you might want to ask that are important to today's Jewish community? For example, why are people still starving? Why is there still fighting in the world?

Why do we ask the same questions every year?

At some Sephardic *Sedarim,* the leader or one of the participants leaves the room after the Four Questions, then returns a few minutes later with a napkin containing the afikoman slung over a shoulder. Everyone at the table then asks: "Who are you?" The person who left the room answers: "A Jew." And the dialogue continues. Questions and answers are exchanged, like: "Where do you come from?" "From Egypt." "What did you do there?" "I was a slave."

Why are the Four Questions not answered immediately?

The four questions in our present-day *Haggadot* are not the same as in those in really old *Haggadot*. One question no longer in use said: On all other nights we eat our meat either boiled or roasted. Why on this night do we eat it roasted? (The roasted meat was a reminder of the roasted paschal lamb that was sacrificed in the Temple.)

# עֲבָדִים הָיִינוּ

## Avadim Hayinu: We Were Slaves

**WHY:** The rabbis have taught us that in order to fully appreciate the Seder experience, we have to relive the life our ancestors lived in Egypt step by step, beginning with slavery and ending with freedom. Here we begin the story of our past by reminding ourselves that we were slaves. For the rabbis, slavery represented both a state of mind and a historical experience. God forcefully brought us out of physical Egypt and through Divine nurturing got it out of our heads too. Even if we already know the story, we tell it again and again. It's all part of being Jewish.

עֲבָדִים הָיִינוּ לְפַרְעֹה בְּמִצְרָיִם, וַיּוֹצִיאֵנוּ יְיָ אֱלֹהֵינוּ מִשָּׁם, בְּיָד חֲזָקָה וּבִזְרוֹעַ נְטוּיָה, וְאִלּוּ לֹא הוֹצִיא, הַקָּדוֹשׁ בָּרוּךְ הוּא, אֶת־אֲבוֹתֵינוּ מִמִּצְרַיִם, הֲרֵי אָנוּ, וּבָנֵינוּ וּבְנֵי בָנֵינוּ, מְשֻׁעְבָּדִים הָיִינוּ לְפַרְעֹה בְּמִצְרָיִם, וַאֲפִלּוּ כֻּלָּנוּ חֲכָמִים, כֻּלָּנוּ נְבוֹנִים, כֻּלָּנוּ זְקֵנִים, כֻּלָּנוּ יוֹדְעִים אֶת־הַתּוֹרָה, מִצְוָה עָלֵינוּ לְסַפֵּר בִּיצִיאַת מִצְרָיִם. וְכָל־הַמַּרְבֶּה לְסַפֵּר בִּיצִיאַת מִצְרַיִם, הֲרֵי זֶה מְשֻׁבָּח:

*We were slaves* to Pharaoh in Mitzrayim, but Adonai our God brought us out of there with a mighty hand and an outstretched arm. Had the Holy Blessed One not taken our ancestors out of Mitzrayim, then we would still be slaves to Pharaoh in Mitzrayim—and so would our children and grandchildren. Even if we were all scholars, sages, elders, or well-versed in Torah, we would still tell the story of the Exodus from Mitzrayim. Everyone who participates in the retelling of the story deserves our attention.

Therefore together we praise God, who was with us in Mitzrayim, who is with us tonight, and who is everywhere.

| | |
|---|---|
| Praised be God who is called Hamakom. | בָּרוּךְ הַמָּקוֹם. |
| | בָּרוּךְ הוּא. |
| Praised be God who gave the Torah to Israel. | בָּרוּךְ שֶׁנָּתַן תּוֹרָה לְעַמּוֹ יִשְׂרָאֵל. |
| Praised be God. | בָּרוּךְ הוּא: |

What is the worst thing about being a slave to anyone?

Let My People Go

When Israel was in Egypt land, let my people go. Oppressed so hard they could not stand, let my people go. Go down, Moses. Way down in Egypt land. Tell old Pharaoh, let my people go.

# אַרְבָּעָה בָּנִים

## Aarbah Banim
## The Four Children

**WHY:** Each of us understands things in a different way. The Four Children represent four different responses to the Seder and different levels of asking questions. So the Seder contains answers to all the ways questions are asked, whether they be deep and profound or simple and straightforward. The wise child (*chacham*) is only interested in knowing what you have to do to make the Seder correctly. The insensitive child (*rasha*) sees the Seder as irrelevant. The uncomplicated child (*tam*) wants to know what the Seder is all about—but just the basics. The young child (*sh'ayno yodeah lishol*) is eager to learn but does not yet know enough to ask.

**HOW TO:** Taking turns, four different people should ask one question each.

What does the wise child ask? "What are the specific things which Adonai asked us to do?" (Deut. 6:20). Tell this child all about the laws of Pesach. This child longs to get closer to God.

What does the insensitive child ask? "What does this stuff have to do with *you*?" (Exod. 12:26). Since this child does not feel a part of the Exodus experience, answer that the Seder is done "because of what Adonai did for *me* when I left Mitzrayim" (Exod. 13:8). We were all there. You and me.

What does the uncomplicated child ask? "What happened? Just tell me the basic story." Reply: "With a mighty hand, Adonai brought us out of Mitzrayim, out of a life of slavery" (Exod. 13:14).

As for the child who does not yet know what to ask, just talk about the Exodus. Tell the whole story from start to finish. The Torah says: "You should explain to your child that we do this because of what Adonai did for me when I left Mitzrayim as a free person" (Exod. 13:8).

What other kinds of kids are there in the world? Regardless of your age, what kind of child are you?

Imagine that you were the wisest child on earth. What advice would you give to your Seder guests?

Talk about a time when you were unable to think of a question to ask. How did you feel?

Add a fifth child who may not be free to celebrate Passover, who asks: "Why can't we celebrate Passover with our fellow Jews?" Have everyone think of a way to help this child. Share it with the others; then go and do it.

## THE BALLAD OF THE FOUR SONS

(To the tune of "Clementine")

1. Said the father to his children
   "At the Seder will you dine,
   You will eat your fill of matzah,
   You will drink four cups of wine."

2. Now this father had no daughters,
   But his sons they numbered four,
   One was wise and one was wicked,
   One was gentle and a bore.

3. And the fourth was sweet and winsome,
   He was young and he was small,
   While his brothers asked the questions
   He could scarcely speak at all.

4. Said the wise son to his father,
   "Would you please explain the laws?
   Of the customs of the Seder
   Will you please explain the cause?"

5. And the father proudly answered,
   "As our fathers ate in speed,
   Ate the Paschal lamb 'ere midnight
   And from slavery were freed.

6. So we follow their example
And 'ere midnight must complete
All the Seder, and we should not
after twelve remain to eat."

7. Then did sneer the son so wicked,
"What does all this mean to you?"
And the father's voice was bitter,
And his grief and anger grew.

8. "If yourself you don't consider
As a son of Israel,
Then for you this has no meaning,
you could be a slave as well."

9. Then the gentle son said gently,
"What is this?" and quietly,
The good father told his offspring,
"We were freed from slavery."

10. But the youngest child was silent,
For he could not ask at all;
His eyes were bright with wonder
as his father told him all.

11. Now, dear children, read the lesson
and remember evermore,
What the father told the children,
Told his sons that numbered four.

## THE FOUR SONS AND THE RAPPERS

Well Hey, you all! Glad you came along
To hear our story told in rhyme and song.
It's about four sons and the questions they raise.
They think about Pesach in different ways.

One son is wise, one argues a lot.
One's got a brain that's really hot.
One's so very young he can't yet speak.
Well, now, let's take a closer peek.

The wise son asks, "What's the meaning and cause
Of all these customs, rules, and laws?"
Since he'll understand the entire story,
The Torah says, "Tell it in all its glory!"

The kid who argues has an attitude.
A Seder just ain't for *this* cool dude.
A Jewish past he says he don't need.
If *he'd* been a slave, he'd never be freed!

The third son's gentle. Keep your story plain.
Long explanations would be inane.
He'll just ask, "What's this?" You can tell him then,
"We escaped from Egypt. We became free men."

Son number four cannot be heard.
The kid's too young—doesn't speak a word.
If you waited for a question, it could take two years.
So begin the story for him. Tell him of our hopes and tears.

Now we sure do hope you enjoyed our rap.
Did it cause you for a moment to put on your thinking cap?
Don't forget, though they were different, from the first to the last son,
Kids are equally important, each and every one.

# וְהִיא שֶׁעָמְדָה

## The V'hee Sh'am-dah

## Promises

**WHY:** Pesach is a holiday which celebrates, among other things, the covenant between God and the Jewish people. God promised Abraham and Sarah, "Know for certain that those who come after you will be strangers in a strange land. They will be afflicted as slaves for four hundred years. But also know that I will judge that nation [Egypt] severely and they will leave as a mighty people" (Gen. 15:13–14). In response, we read the V'hi She'amda passage.

**HOW TO:** Cover the matzah and raise your cup of wine. After you have said the following V'hi She'amda, place your cup back on the table and uncover the matzah once again.

וְהִיא שֶׁעָמְדָה לַאֲבוֹתֵינוּ וְלָנוּ. שֶׁלֹּא אֶחָד בִּלְבָד, עָמַד עָלֵינוּ לְכַלּוֹתֵנוּ. אֶלָּא שֶׁבְּכָל דּוֹר וָדוֹר, עוֹמְדִים עָלֵינוּ לְכַלּוֹתֵנוּ. וְהַקָּדוֹשׁ בָּרוּךְ הוּא מַצִּילֵנוּ מִיָּדָם:

It is the promise to our ancestors and to us that still holds true. Not just one enemy has arisen to destroy us. Instead, in every generation there are people who have tried to destroy us, but the Holy Blessed One has saved us from their hands.

# צֵא וּלְמַד

## Tze Ul'mad: Come and Learn

**WHY:** This part of the Seder fills in the gaps in the story. We now know that the Israelites were slaves in Egypt and that God, through Moses' leadership, guided us out of Egypt. But how did we become slaves in the first place? How did Moses become such an important leader of the Jewish people? And how did Moses actually get all those people out of Egypt without being stopped by the Egyptian army? For the answers, we have to go all the way back to Joseph.

**HOW TO:** Let's read the story together. Begin by reading the Torah text that tells it all.

אֲרַמִּי אֹבֵד אָבִי, וַיֵּרֶד מִצְרַיְמָה, וַיָּגָר שָׁם בִּמְתֵי מְעָט. וַיְהִי־שָׁם לְגוֹי גָּדוֹל, עָצוּם וָרָב:

וַיָּרֵעוּ אֹתָנוּ הַמִּצְרִים וַיְעַנּוּנוּ. וַיִּתְּנוּ עָלֵינוּ עֲבֹדָה קָשָׁה:

וַנִּצְעַק אֶל־יְיָ אֱלֹהֵי אֲבֹתֵינוּ, וַיִּשְׁמַע יְיָ אֶת־קֹלֵנוּ, וַיַּרְא אֶת־עָנְיֵנוּ, וְאֶת־עֲמָלֵנוּ, וְאֶת־לַחֲצֵנוּ:

וַיּוֹצִאֵנוּ יְיָ מִמִּצְרַיִם, בְּיָד חֲזָקָה, וּבִזְרֹעַ נְטוּיָה, וּבְמֹרָא גָּדֹל. וּבְאֹתוֹת וּבְמֹפְתִים:

My ancestor was a nomad from a place called Aram Naharayim. With only a few people, he went down to Mitzrayim and lived there. There my ancestors became a great nation, mighty and numerous. The Egyptians were cruel to us and they forced us to work for them as slaves. We cried out to Adonai, the God of our ancestors. God heard our cry and took note of our painful life. So with an outstretched arm, with awesome power, and with incredible signs of Divine wonder, Adonai took us out of Mitzrayim.

(Deut. 26:5–8)

# Hunger in the Land

There was famine in the land of Canaan, so Jacob sent his sons to get food in Egypt. Thinking that their brother Joseph was a slave (since they had sold him into slavery), they were surprised to learn that he had become the prime minister. Joseph's family joined him in Egypt, where they lived for a long time. Then Joseph died, and after several generations the Egyptian people forgot how Joseph had saved their nation from dying of starvation. It was he who had the idea to store food during good farming years so that it would be available when the farmers were not able to produce enough food for everyone. Not only did the new Pharaoh of Egypt forget what Joseph had done but he was afraid that the Israelites were growing too strong. They had big families and were influential members of society. So the Pharaoh made them slaves.

# Egyptian Slavery

But that was still not enough. Pharaoh needed a way to prevent the slaves from growing too strong, making sure that there would not be too many of them. So he cruelly decided to have all the baby Israelite boys killed at birth. This would be done by the midwives—the women who helped those who were giving birth. But two of the midwives, whose names were Shifrah and Puah, refused to do it. And the Israelite women devised ways of protecting their children.

## Moses' Birthday

One woman, Yocheved, put her new son in a little straw basket and floated him down the Nile River, praying that he would be safe. She sent her daughter Miriam to look after the little boy. Meanwhile, Pharaoh's grown daughter was bathing in the river. She found the infant, adopted him, and named him Moses. Miriam ran and got her mother, who volunteered to be a wetnurse for the young boy. While tending little Moses, his natural mother Yocheved taught him the ways of the Israelites. At the same time, Pharaoh's daughter raised him as the Pharaoh's grandson, a prince, a member of the Egyptian royal family.

## Moses Grows Up

Moses always knew he was different. He didn't like seeing bullies beating up on other people. Once, when he saw an Egyptian taskmaster whipping an Israelite slave, he couldn't stand it anymore and rescued the Israelite slave. Afraid for his own life because of what he had done, Moses fled to the desert to a place called Midian. He lived there with a shepherd named Jethro and eventually married one of Jethro's daughters, Zipporah.

One day, Moses was out tending Jethro's flock when he saw an incredible thing happen. A bush appeared to be on fire but its branches were not being burned. And he heard God speak: "Moses, take off your shoes. You are on holy ground." And God told Moses to go to Pharaoh and tell him, "Let My people go." Moses was afraid to go alone. He did not speak well. So God told Moses to take his brother Aaron with him. Moses felt God's presence, and that's what really gave him the courage to face Pharaoh and demand the release of the Israelites from slavery.

# Let My People Go

Moses went to Pharaoh, who was not easy to convince. Moses demonstrated God's power, but this made Pharaoh very angry. How dare Moses make demands! And so, Pharaoh made things even worse for the Israelite slaves and made them suffer even more.

During the Magid section of the Passover Seder we retell the story of our brothers and sisters in Egypt. Imagine now that you were there and fill in your own memories of the story.

A long time ago my family were slaves in Egypt. Our house in Egypt was very ______. I remember playing with ______, but most of the time I would have to go to work. When I went to work I remember ______. The first time I met King Pharaoh I thought ______. All the kids used to say that Pharaoh would ______. One day Moses came to our people and said ______. I could hardly believe it, but I decided ______. When the plagues finally came I felt ______. The plague I will never forget is the one that __________. When we left Egypt my family took three things with them. They were __________, __________, and __________. The one thing I most remember about the matzah when we left Egypt was ______. When we reached the Red Sea I looked at it and felt ____. When Moses raised his hand and rod, and the sea split, I ______.
When we crossed the Red Sea I felt like singing ______. All in all I will never ever forget __________. When I have my own family I will always make sure to tell them ______.

Place a small bucket of water on the floor and have participants jump over it to remind them of the crossing of the Red Sea.

During this section, when the Israelites finally leave Egypt, the Caucasus Mountain Jews raise their hands toward heaven and say, "May it be the will of God that the Messiah, the son of David, rescue all people in exile, as Adonai our God rescued our ancestors in times of old."

## A Place for Seder Thoughts of My Own

# הַמַּכּוֹת

## Ha-makot

## The Plagues

**WHY:** Pharaoh was not persuaded by Moses' first attempt to get him to free the Israelites. And so, God wanted to show Pharaoh who he was dealing with. The plagues sound cruel, and they were. But so was the slavery the Israelites were forced to endure. Each time God brought a plague on the Egyptians, it seemed that Pharaoh was going to free the Israelites. But each time Pharaoh survived a plague, he changed his mind and made things even worse for them. Until the last plague crushed even Pharaoh's iron will.

**HOW TO:** Read the plagues one at a time. Each time you read a plague, dip your little finger in your cup of wine and place a droplet on your plate. Don't lick your finger; these are plagues!

| | | |
|---|---|---|
| Blood | **Dam.** | 1) דָּם. |
| Frogs | **Tz'far-dey-a.** | 2) צְפַרְדֵּעַ. |
| Lice | **Ki-nim.** | 3) כִּנִּים. |
| Flies | **A- rov.** | 4) עָרוֹב. |
| Cattle Disease | **De-ver.** | 5) דֶּבֶר. |
| Boils | **Sh'chin.** | 6) שְׁחִין. |
| Hail | **Ba-rad.** | 7) בָּרָד. |
| Locusts | **Arbeh.** | 8) אַרְבֶּה. |
| Darkness | **Cho-shech.** | 9) חֹשֶׁךְ. |
| Death of the Firstborn | **Ma-kat B'chorot.** | 10) מַכַּת בְּכוֹרוֹת: |

Some say that Rabbi Yehudah wanted to help us remember the plagues. Others say he could not bring himself to list the plagues because of the pain they had caused the Egyptians. Remember the order of the plagues the way Rabbi Yehudah taught us.

D'TZaCH ADaSH B'ACHaV

דְּצַ"ךְ עֲדַ"שׁ בְּאַחַ"ב:

What are some other plagues you can think of that have created problems in our world? Go around the Seder table and ask each person to share an original modern-day plague with the group. Be ready to explain why it is a plague.

Use props as visual aids to enhance the plagues: e.g., rubber frogs, food coloring that will turn water red, plastic insects, small foam balls for hail, etc. Use your imagination. Be as creative as you've always wanted to be.

Some people tilt their glasses of wine and pour out a little each time, "lessening our joy."

Here are the ten plagues in pictures. Can you put them in the proper order?

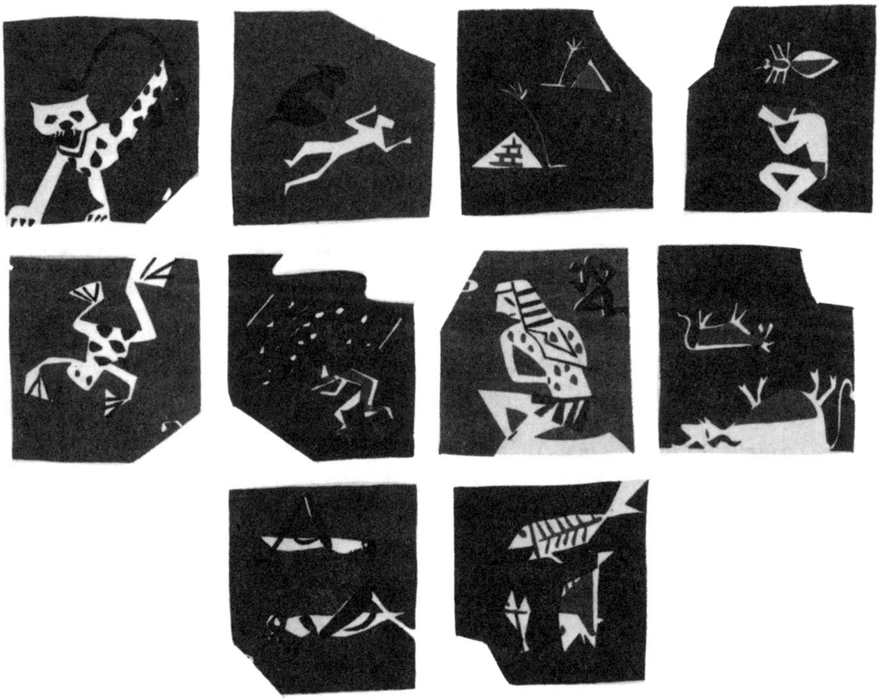

# דַּיֵּנוּ

## Dayenu:
## It Would Have Been Enough

**WHY:** Often, when we look for a way to thank God, we start singing. This well-known song expresses thanks to God for everything God did for us during the Exodus. The chorus says it all: Dayenu—it would have been enough. Now it's time for us to do the rest.

**HOW TO:** Sing the three important verses of the song and don't forget the chorus. They are listed first. Keep the chorus going and going and going. Then read through the remainder of the verses. Don't forget to keep the chorus going strong.

| | |
|---|---|
| Ilu hotzianu miMitzrayim. | אִלּוּ הוֹצִיאָנוּ מִמִּצְרַיִם, |
| Dayenu. | דַּיֵּנוּ: |
| Ilu natan lanu et haShabbat. | אִלּוּ נָתַן לָנוּ אֶת הַשַּׁבָּת, |
| Dayenu. | דַּיֵּנוּ: |
| Ilu natan lanu et haTorah. | אִלּוּ נָתַן לָנוּ אֶת־הַתּוֹרָה, |
| Dayenu. | דַּיֵּנוּ: |

God brought us out of Egypt. Dayenu.
Punished the Egyptians and destroyed their idols. Dayenu.
Divided the Red Sea for us so that we could cross on dry land. Dayenu.
Nurtured us in the desert for forty years by feeding us heavenly manna. Dayenu.
Gave us Shabbat. Dayenu.
Brought us to Mount Sinai and gave us Torah. Dayenu.
Brought us to the Promised Land, to Eretz Yisrael. Dayenu.
Built the ancient Temple. Dayenu.
For each of these things and for all of them together, we sing DAYENU.

Dayenu means "it would have been enough?" Try to answer some modern "is it enough?" questions.

1. Is it enough for us to read a Jewish book but not study Torah?
2. Is it enough for us to recite "let all who are hungry come and eat" without going out and feeding the hungry?

Fill in the blanks.

1. Is it enough for us to attend a Jewish rally without _____?
2. Is it enough for us to celebrate a Seder without _______?
3. Is it enough for us to be upset with violence in the world without ________?

In some German *Haggadot* there is a direction for the matzah balls to be thrown into the soup after the chanting of Dayenu.

Some people sing Dayenu as a question: "Is it enough?" For example, if God had fed us manna without giving us the Shabbat, would it be enough? Here are some modern Dayenu questions which you may want to include in your Seder:

Is it enough to give tzedakah (charity) but not personally offer to help? Dayenu?

Is it enough to pray and not to follow through on the values in the prayerbook? Dayenu?

# פֶּסַח

## Pesach: The Mezuzah Bone

**WHY:** This symbol is tied to the name of the holiday. It represents the critical moment in the Passover story. After the final plague Pharaoh gave in—his own son had been killed. To prevent the plague from reaching the Israelite households, blood from the spring offering was placed on the doorposts about the same place we put out mezuzot. We point to the bone to make sure everyone remembers what happened.

**HOW TO:** Point to the lamb bone (or red beet if you are a vegetarian) and explain what happened in your own words. Here is the way it is written in the Torah:

"You should tell them, 'It is the Pesach offering to Adonai because God passed over the Israelite homes in Egypt, when the Egyptians were killed and our homes were protected' " (Exod. 12:27).

### A Place for Seder Thoughts of My Own

# בְּכָל־דּוֹר וָדוֹר

## B'chol Dor Vador: In Every Generation

**WHY:** The Haggadah is not just a book of stories from the distant past. It is a living record of Jewish history which we add to each year as we participate in the Seder. We all feel part of Jewish history, from the Exodus to the giving of the Torah unto today. And so, we read this section to remind ourselves of our obligation.

**HOW TO:** Many melodies have been written for this text. Choose the one you like or just read it in a traditional chant. Sing it through several times until it flows from your lips into your heart and soul.

| | |
|---|---|
| In every generation, individuals should look upon themselves as if personally freed from Mitzrayim. | בְּכָל־דּוֹר וָדוֹר חַיָּב אָדָם לִרְאוֹת אֶת־עַצְמוֹ, כְּאִלּוּ הוּא יָצָא מִמִּצרים. |

**B'chol dor vador cha-yav adam lir-ot et atz-moh, k'illoo hoo yah-tzah m'mitzrayim.**

Why do you think Rabban Gamliel chose Pesach, Matzah, and Maror as the three most important symbols for the Seder?

If you could choose the most important three symbols, what would they be and why?

In this part of the Seder we are reminded that we must feel as if we were in Egypt and were personally freed. Imagine what it was like not to be free. Talk about what it was like when you were a slave in Egypt. Also, share one of the first things you would have done once you were free from the Egyptians.

When Sephardim say B'chol Dor Vador, "In every generation we must feel that we ourselves personally left Egypt," participants pick up green onions or scallions and beat each other on the back and shoulders. It is a reminder of the whipping that the slaves received in Egypt. Go ahead and try it.

# הַלְלוּיָהּ

## Halleluyah!

**WHY:** Psalms 113 to 118 are recited at this point in the Seder. They thank God for all of the things God did for us. They are called the Egyptian Hallel because, so the rabbis tell us, these very psalms were chanted by the Israelites at the Red Sea. And that's where we are in the story.

**HOW TO:** So let's listen to the next part of the story. But let's begin with two psalms from the Egyptian Hallel.

Halleluyah. Those who worship Adonai, sing praises. From the rising of the sun until its setting. May the name of Adonai be praised now and forever.

(from Psalm 113)

בְּצֵאת יִשְׂרָאֵל מִמִּצְרָיִם
בֵּית יַעֲקֹב מֵעַם לֹעֵז: הָיְתָה
יְהוּדָה לְקָדְשׁוֹ יִשְׂרָאֵל
מַמְשְׁלוֹתָיו: הַיָּם רָאָה וַיָּנֹס
הַיַּרְדֵּן יִסֹּב לְאָחוֹר: הֶהָרִים
רָקְדוּ כְאֵילִים גְּבָעוֹת כִּבְנֵי־
צֹאן: מַה־לְּךָ הַיָּם כִּי תָנוּס
הַיַּרְדֵּן תִּסֹּב לְאָחוֹר: הֶהָרִים
תִּרְקְדוּ כְאֵילִים גְּבָעוֹת
כִּבְנֵי־צֹאן: מִלִּפְנֵי אָדוֹן
חוּלִי אָרֶץ מִלִּפְנֵי אֱלוֹהַּ
יַעֲקֹב: הַהֹפְכִי הַצּוּר אֲגַם־
מָיִם חַלָּמִישׁ לְמַעְיְנוֹ־מָיִם:

When the Israelites left Egypt, they became the holy Jewish people. During their journey, the sea washed away from the shore and the Jordan River ran backwards. Mountains looked like rams skipping. Even the earth shook. All because they felt the presence of the God of Jacob in their midst, who turns the rock into a pool of water, the flint into a flowing fountain.

(from Psalm 114)

## Miriam's Song

And the women dancing with their
timbrels
Followed Miriam as she sang her song
Sing a song to the One whom we've
exalted
Miriam and the women danced and
danced the whole night long.

Miriam was a weaver of unique variety
The tapestry she wove was one which
sang our history
With every strand and every thread she
crafted her delight
A woman touched with spirit she dances
toward the light. *Chorus:*

When Miriam stood upon the shores and
gazed across the sea
The wonder of this miracle she soon
came to believe
Whoever thought the sea would part with
an outstretched hand
And we would pass to freedom and march
to the promised land? *Chorus:*

And Miriam the prophet took the timbrel
in her hand
And all the women followed her just as
she had planned
And Miriam raised her voice in song, she
sang with praise and might
We've just lived through a miracle, we're
going to dance tonight.

When it was finally time the Israelites left quickly and ran toward the Red Sea. Pharaoh sent his army after them, angry at what had happened. And the Israelites were at the shore of the sea. Moses didn't know what to do. The Israelites were afraid to cross, until one man took the fateful plunge and jumped into the water. Moses raised his staff and the Red Sea parted. The Israelites crossed onto dry land. The waters returned as the Egyptian army was pursuing the Israelites—and all the soldiers were drowned.

Miriam, Moses' sister, led the Israelites in song and dance, thankful that they had been saved and were finally free.

# כּוֹס שְׁנִיָּה

## Kos Shnee-yah
## The Second Cup

**WHY:** This cup of wine is for the second promise God made to our ancestors. "I will deliver you from slavery" (Exod. 6:6).

**HOW TO:** Raise your cup while reciting the blessing. Then you may drink the second cup. ~~Lean on your arm when drinking. Remember to get comfortable.~~

Heneni muchan u'mizuman. I am ready to fulfill the mitzvah of drinking the second cup of wine.

הִנְנִי מוּכָן וּמְזֻמָּן לְקַיֵּם מִצְוַת כּוֹס שְׁנִיָּה

Praised are You, Adonai, who has freed our people. Praised are You, Adonai our God, Guide of the Universe, who creates the fruit that grows on the vine.

בָּרוּךְ אַתָּה יְיָ, אֱלֹהֵינוּ מֶלֶךְ הָעוֹלָם, בּוֹרֵא, פְּרִי הַגָּפֶן:

**Ba-ruch a-tah A-do-nai, E-lo-hey-nu melech ha-o-lam, bo-rey p'-ri ha-ga-fen.**

# רָחְצָה

## Rachtzah: Cleansing

**WHY:** Now we are getting ready to eat. We want to make sure that our hands are ritually clean—the same way the ancient priests washed their hands before preparing a sacrifice. As a holy people, we all become priests and our Seder table becomes an altar.

**HOW TO:** Use a pitcher or a cup and pour water over your hands two or three times; then recite the blessing.

Praised are You, Adonai our God, Guide of the Universe, who made us special through mitzvot and instructed us to wash our hands.

בָּרוּךְ אַתָּה יְיָ, אֱלֹהֵינוּ מֶלֶךְ הָעוֹלָם, אֲשֶׁר קִדְּשָׁנוּ בְּמִצְוֹתָיו, וְצִוָּנוּ עַל-נְטִילַת יָדָיִם:

**Ba-ruch a-tah A-do-nai, E-lo-hey-nu me-lech ha-o-lam, a-sher kid-sha-nu b'-mitz-vo-tav v'-tzi-va-nu al n'-ti-lat ya-da-yim.**

Why do you think we say a blessing when we wash our hands this time? Remember, we didn't say a blessing the first time (during Urchatz).

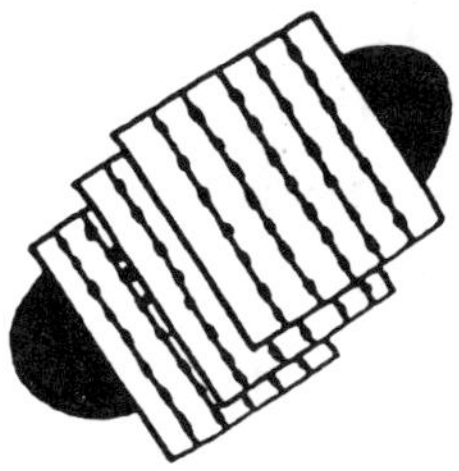

# מוֹצִיא מַצָּה

## Motzi Matzah:
## Eating Matzah "Bread"

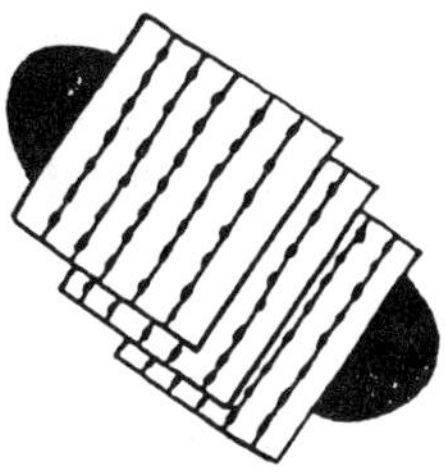

**WHY:** Bread is a symbol for all of the things we eat on a regular basis. It is a staple of the diet in our part of the world (in other places, rice serves the same purpose). Since we are about to eat—note that our hands are ritually clean—we say a blessing of thanks to God for bread and then for the special matzah bread we are taught to eat for the week of Pesach.

**HOW TO:** Lift the three pieces of matzah (really two and one-half pieces!) and recite the following two blessings, one for bread (which includes matzah) and one just for matzah. After you say the blessings, pass out pieces of the upper and middle *matzot* for eating. It's OK to eat the matzah now, but only if you are still relaxing. Don't eat the bottom piece. We have to save it for later.

Praised are You, Adonai our God, Guide of the Universe, who makes bread grow from the earth.

בָּרוּךְ אַתָּה יְיָ, אֱלֹהֵינוּ מֶלֶךְ הָעוֹלָם, הַמּוֹצִיא לֶחֶם מִן־הָאָרֶץ:

**Ba-ruch a-tah A-do-nai, E-lo-hey-nu me-lech ha-o-lam, ha-mo-tzi le-chem min ha-a-retz.**

Praised are You, Adonai our God, Guide of the Universe, who made us special through mitzvot and instructed us to eat matzah.

בָּרוּךְ אַתָּה יְיָ, אֱלֹהֵינוּ מֶלֶךְ הָעוֹלָם, אֲשֶׁר קִדְּשָׁנוּ בְּמִצְוֹתָיו, וְצִוָּנוּ עַל־אֲכִילַת מַצָּה:

**Ba-ruch a-tah A-do-nai, E-lo-hey-nu me-lech ha-o-lam, a-sher kid-sha-nu b'mitz-vo-tav v'-tzi-va-nu al a-chi-lat ma-tzah.**

What are the two earliest biblical stories that describe matzah being served? Hint: Read Genesis chapters 18 and 19. Why is the Motzi (the prayer over bread) also said over matzah?

During Passover 1944 there was no matzah in the Bergen-Belsen concentration camp. The rabbis there said that the Jewish prisoners would be allowed to eat chametz, knowing full well that if they did not they would die of starvation. The rabbis further said that a special prayer for chametz would have to be recited. This was the prayer: "Our Father, it is known to You that it is our wish to do Your will and to celebrate Passover by eating matzah and not eating chametz. But our heart is pained because our enslavement prevents us and we are in danger of our lives. Behold, we are ready to fulfill Your mitzvah: 'And you shall live by My laws, and not die by them.' We pray to You that You may keep us alive and redeem us soon so that we may observe Your laws and serve You with a perfect heart. Amen."

During the time of the Talmud, matzah was made with designs on it. The designs included pictures of doves, fish, and flowers.

The first matzah-making machine was invented in Austria in the late 1850s. During the Middle Ages matzot were thick, even thicker than a bagel, and circular in shape.

In New York City an estimate of the total Jewish population in 1859 was made on the basis of matzah production. Figuring an average of 5 pounds per person, it was calculated that at least 40,000 Jewish people lived in New York.

Did you know that the Egyptians were one of the first cultures to learn how to use yeast to make bread rise? Since yeast is chametz, perhaps that is why eating *any* yeast product on Pesach is prohibited.

# מָרוֹר

## Maror: Bitter Horseradish

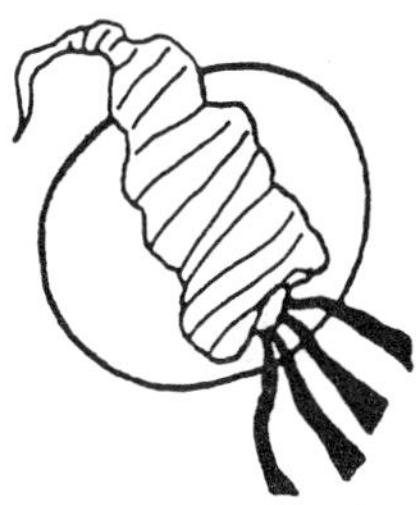

**WHY:** This herb reminds us how bitter were the lives our ancestors lived as slaves. We want to feel their pain throughout our bodies, so it's not enough just to think it, say it, or even feel it. We want to be able to actually taste their pain. The charoset we eat looks a little like the mortar the Israelite slaves used to cement bricks together when they were forced to build the Egyptian cities of Pithom and Raamses.

**HOW TO:** Point to the horseradish. Dip it in the charoset. (This is the second time we dip our vegetables.) Say the blessing; then you can eat it—or at least try to eat it.

Praised are You, Adonai our God, Guide of the Universe who made us special through mitzvot and instructed us to eat maror.

בָּרוּךְ אַתָּה יְיָ, אֱלֹהֵינוּ מֶלֶךְ הָעוֹלָם, אֲשֶׁר קִדְּשָׁנוּ בְּמִצְוֹתָיו, וְצִוָּנוּ עַל־אֲכִילַת מָרוֹר.

**Ba-ruch a-tah A-do-nai, E-lo-hey-nu me-leh ha-o-lam, a-sher kid-sha-nu b'-mitz-vo-tav v'-tzi-va-nu al a-chi-lat ma-ror.**

Maror means "bitter things." Talk about all of the things that make you feel bitter. Share some solutions and ways of making bitter things sweet again.

9

# כּוֹרֵךְ

## Korech:
## Hillel's Sandwich

**WHY:** Out of respect for our great teacher Hillel, we eat this peculiar sandwich which combines all of the ingredients of the bitterness of slavery. Hillel taught us that this is the way that people ate the Pesach (remember the shankbone) during the time of the ancient Temple: with matzah and maror.

**HOW TO:** Distribute pieces from the bottom matzah (the only one left from the original three). Make a charoset-and-horseradish sandwich for each person. Just eat the sandwich. No blessing is needed because we have already said the blessings for both matzah and maror.

The Earl of Sandwich has always been considered the inventor of the sandwich. Did you know that Hillel really created the first sandwich when he put matzah and maror together and ate them as a sandwich almost 2,000 years ago?

Moroccan Jews grind dates and nuts into balls for charoset. Iraqi Jews make a syrup of dates. Turkish Jews add raisins and orange peel. Yemenites add grains.

# שֻׁלְחָן עוֹרֵךְ

## Shulchan Orech:
## The Meal Is Served

**WHY:** We begin our meal with an egg because an egg is a symbol of new life. This is the new life the Israelites enjoyed after they were freed from Egypt. Some say that we use hardboiled eggs because the more you boil an egg the harder it gets. The Israelites were the same way. The more that Pharaoh punished them, the stronger and more numerous they became.

**HOW TO:** We know that we don't have to tell you how to eat. However, many people begin the meal with a hardboiled egg dipped in salt water. ~~(Since this is a custom for some families but not all, it's not considered a third dipping. Otherwise, we'd have to change the Four Questions!)~~ Enjoy!

*Game of Odds and Evens.* Give out nuts to each participant. Ask them to hold the nuts in their hands. Going around the Seder table, the others have to guess whether the number of nuts in a person's hand is an even or an odd number.

*Initial Game.* Have some initials prewritten on index cards and ask participants to guess what they stand for. For example,

| | |
|---|---|
| 5 B of M | (Five Books of Moses) |
| 8 D of P | (8 Days of Passover) |
| 4 Q | (4 Questions) |
| 4 C of W | (4 Cups of Wine) |

*Scrambled Words.* Prepare some Passover-related words on index cards. The letters of each word are scrambled. Have the family leader hold up each card and ask participants to try to guess the word. Here are a few to get you started.

ATZMAH (Matzah)
NEWI (Wine)
REEFMOD (Freedom)

*Match Game*. The family leader reads each of the following statements and participants fill in the blanks with their own clever answers.

a. Dum Dora was so dumb that she made her matzah balls using matzah meal and ______.
b. Did you hear about the new Passover yo yo? When you throw it, it always ______.
c. Orthodox scientists are working on a new food creation for Passover. It's called a matzah ______.
d. Madeline's matzah balls were so hard that when you put them on a spoon they ______.
e. They just found an ancient Haggadah with a fifteenth part of the Seder. It occurs at the end of the book and it's called ______.

*Ashkenazim* avoid lamb as a main course at the Seder because it was used as a sacrifice in the Temple. *Sephardim* generally eat lamb to commemorate the night of the Exodus.

*Broken Telephone*. Prepare some Passover-related sentences on index cards. The family leader whispers the sentence to the person sitting in the next seat, and each person in turn whispers the sentence to the next person, and so on down the line. The last person then says the sentence. Try these sentences to get you started.

a. The angel of God passed over the houses of the Israelites and they were saved from death.
b. God brought us out from Egypt with a strong arm and an outstretched hand.

# צָפוּן

## Tzafun: The Hidden Afikoman

**WHY:** In order to make sure that slavery is the last thing you taste during your Seder, nothing is eaten after the afikoman is shared by the participants. (But we do have two more cups of wine to go.) This assumes that you have found the afikoman, of course! The afikoman is a kind of dessert. In the days of the ancient Temple, the Pesach offering was the last thing eaten at the Seder. Now that the Temple is gone, the afikoman serves as a symbol of the offering. It too is the last thing eaten at the Seder. Since we are no longer hungry but we eat it anyway, it is holy eating.

**HOW TO:** The afikoman (the piece of the middle matzah broken during Yachatz) has been hidden since early in the Seder. Now go and look for it. After you have received a "finder's fee," break it into pieces and share it with everyone else.

Why do you think that hiding and finding things are part of the Passover Seder?

Play the Afikoman Game. The participants sing a Passover song while the "searchers" look for the afikoman. As the searcher gets closer to the afikoman, those at the Seder table sing the song more loudly. As the searcher moves away from the afikoman, progressively sing more softly.

# בָּרֵךְ

## Barech: Giving Thanks

**WHY:** Just as we thanked God for food before we ate our meal, we now thank God after the meal with the traditional grace, Birkat Hamazon.

**HOW TO:** If there are three people present, include the introductory section, which is an invitation to join in. If ten people have joined you, say the word "God" (given in parentheses) instead of "the One." We have included the short form of the prayer. Now is also the time to get ready to drink the third cup of wine, so go ahead and fill it up before you recite Birkat Hamazon.

*Leader:* Friends, let's give thanks.

חֲבֵרַי נְבָרֵךְ:

**Cha-vey-rai n'-va-reych.**

*Friends:* May Adonai be praised forever.

יְהִי שֵׁם יְיָ מְבֹרָךְ מֵעַתָּה
וְעַד עוֹלָם:

**Y'-hi sheym A-do-nai m'-vo rach mey-a-ta v'-ad o-lam.**

*Leader:* With your permission, my friends and teachers who are present, let's praise the One (God) whose food we have eaten.

בִּרְשׁוּת מָרָנָן וְרַבָּנָן
וְחַבֵרַי, נְבָרֵךְ (אֱלֹהֵינוּ)
שֶׁאָכַלְנוּ מִשֶּׁלּוֹ:

**Bir-shut ma-ra-nan v'rab-bannan, v'-cha-vey-rai n'-va-reych (El-lo-hey-nu) she-a-chal-nu mi-she-lo.**

*Friends:* Praised be the One (God) whose food we have eaten and whose goodness we enjoy.

בָּרוּךְ (אֱלֹהֵינוּ) שֶׁאָכַלְנוּ מִשֶּׁלּוֹ וּבְטוּבוֹ חָיִינוּ:

**Ba-ruch (E-lo-hey-nu) she-a-chal-nu mi-she-lo uv-tu-vo cha-yi-nu.**

*Leader and Friends:* Praised be Adonai. And praised be the holy name.

בָּרוּךְ הוּא וּבָרוּךְ שְׁמוֹ:

Praised is Adonai our God, Guide of the Universe, who nourishes the entire world out of divine goodness and grace and with mercy. You provide food to all because Your mercy is unending.

בָּרוּךְ אַתָּה יְיָ, אֱלֹהֵינוּ מֶלֶךְ הָעוֹלָם, הַזָּן אֶת־הַכֹּל.

Your goodness has caused us never to be in want for food. All this for the sake of Your great name. You provide for all. You nurture all by providing food for all the creatures You have created. Praised is Adonai, who provides food for all. Quickly build holy Jerusalem in our time. Praised be Adonai, who out of mercy rebuilds Jerusalem. I have been young and now I am old. Never have I seen the righteous so forsaken that their children are forced to beg for food. May the One who makes peace in high places make peace for us, for all the Jewish people, and for all people. Grant strength to your people. Bless Your people with peace.

The blessing after the meal says thank you to God for our food. Talk about three other things for which you want to thank God.

# כּוֹס שְׁלִישִׁית

## Kos Sh'lee-sheet
## The Third Cup

**WHY:** This time we drink wine to remember the third of God's promises to bring us out of Egypt: "I will rescue you with an outstretched arm and incredible decisions" (Exod. 6:6).

**HOW TO:** Lift up your cup and recite the blessing. Then, while still leaning on your side, drink your third cup.

הִנְנִי מוּכָן וּמְזֻמָּן לְקַיֵּם מִצְוַת כּוֹס שְׁלִישִׁית.

Heneni muchan u'mizuman. I am ready to fulfill the mitzvah of drinking the third cup of wine.

בָּרוּךְ אַתָּה יְיָ, אֱלֹהֵינוּ מֶלֶךְ הָעוֹלָם, בּוֹרֵא, פְּרִי הַגָּפֶן:

Praised are You, Adonai our God, Guide of the Universe, who creates fruit that grows on the vine.

**Ba-ruch a-tah A-do-nai, E-lo-hey-nu melech ha-o-lam, bo-rey p'-ri ha-ga-fen.**

# אֵלִיָּהוּ הַנָּבִיא

## Eliahu Hanavi: Welcoming Elijah the Prophet

**WHY:** According to Jewish tradition, Elijah the Prophet is the one who will announce that the messianic era is coming. It's a big word for a big time! Since the Seder is a time when we celebrate freedom and liberty, we wait and hope for Elijah to come and announce the ultimate in freedom and liberty.

**HOW TO:** Fill up Elijah's cup. Some people do it by adding a little wine from their own cups as they fill their cups now to prepare for the fourth cup (which we will drink later). Send someone to open the front door while you read the following passages. Don't forget to close the door afterwards!

Pour out Your anger on those who do not know You, on all those governments that do not cry out to You. They have destroyed the dwelling place of the people of Jacob, now called Israel.

(Psalms 79:6–7)

שְׁפֹךְ חֲמָתְךָ אֶל־הַגּוֹיִם אֲשֶׁר לֹא־יְדָעוּךָ, וְעַל־מַמְלָכוֹת אֲשֶׁר בְּשִׁמְךָ לֹא קָרָאוּ: כִּי אָכַל אֶת־יַעֲקֹב וְאֶת־נָוֵהוּ הֵשַׁמּוּ:

Eliyahu haNavi, Eliyahu haTishbi
Eliyahu, Eliyahu, Eliyahu haGiladi
Bimhera v'yameinu yavo eleinu im Mashiach ben David

אֵלִיָּהוּ הַנָּבִיא, אֵלִיָּהוּ הַתִּשְׁבִּי,
אֵלִיָּהוּ, אֵלִיָּהוּ, אֵלִיָּהוּ הַגִּלְעָדִי.
בִּמְהֵרָה בְיָמֵינוּ, יָבֹא אֵלֵינוּ.
עִם מָשִׁיחַ בֶּן דָּוִד, עִם מָשִׁיחַ בֶּן דָּוִד.

May Elijah the Prophet come quickly in our day and bring the time of the Messiah.

How can you help God feed the world? What will the world look like when the Messiah comes?

Have someone dress up as Elijah and wait outside at the door.

Pass around Elijah's cup and have each person pour some of their wine into it, symbolizing cooperation toward working for peace.

Yemenite Jews do not use the Elijah's cup.

## A Place for Seder Thoughts of My Own

13

# הַלֵּל

# Hallel: Songs of Praise

**WHY:** The word "Hallel" means "praise." It is the name for a group of psalms (115–118) that the Levites sang in the ancient Jerusalem Temple. The Hallel psalms all thank God for the many things God has done for the Jewish people. We recited two of the Hallel psalms before the meal. Now we say the rest of them. We divide the Hallel so that we can include the meal as part of our way of singing praise to God.

**HOW TO:** This section concludes with the drinking of the fourth cup. Some people include songs at this time in the Seder also, after Hallel, before the fourth cup.

Adonai remembers us with blessing.
God will bless the house of Israel.
God will bless the house of Aaron.
Blessed are you who honor Adonai,
  both the young and the old.
May Adonai send you and your children blessings.
May you be blessed by Adonai,
the One who creates heaven and earth.
The heavens are the heavens of Adonai,
but the earth was given to humans.
The dead cannot sing Halleluyah.
Those who are silent cannot praise God.
So we praise God now and forever. Halleluyah.

(from Psalm 115)

Praise Adonai, all you nations; praise God, all you peoples. For God's acts of kindness are great and the truth of Adonai is forever. Halleluyah.

הַלְלוּ אֶת־יְיָ כָּל־גּוֹיִם,
שַׁבְּחוּהוּ כָּל־הָאֻמִּים: כִּי גָבַר
עָלֵינוּ חַסְדּוֹ, וֶאֱמֶת־יְיָ לְעוֹלָם,
הַלְלוּיָהּ:

(from Psalm 117)

Give thanks to Adonai, for all is good.
God's kindness is forever.
Israel should say:
God's kindness is forever.
The House of Aaron should say:
God's kindness is forever.
Everyone who reveres God should say:
God's kindness is forever.

הוֹדוּ לַייָ כִּי־טוֹב,
כִּי לְעוֹלָם חַסְדּוֹ.
יֹאמַר־נָא יִשְׂרָאֵל,
כִּי לְעוֹלָם חַסְדּוֹ.
יֹאמְרוּ־נָא בֵית־אַהֲרֹן,
כִּי לְעוֹלָם חַסְדּוֹ.
יֹאמְרוּ־נָא יִרְאֵי יְיָ,
כִּי לְעוֹלָם חַסְדּוֹ.

(from Psalm 118)

**Ho-du l'A-do-nai ki tov**
**Kee l'-o-lam chas-do**
**Yo-mar-na Yis-ra-el**
**Kee l'-o-lam chas-do**
**Yom-ru-na bet A-ḥa-ron**
**Kee l'-o-lam chas-do**
**Yom-ru-na yir-ay A-do-nai**
**Kee l'-o-lam chas-do**

God has many different names, and each one tells us something special about God. Fill in the blanks:

God is called a Rock because ________________.
God is called our Parent because ________________.
God is called our Shepherd because ________________.

# נִשְׁמַת כָּל־חַי

## Nishmat Kol Chai: All Living Things

**WHY:** This songlike prayer is said every Shabbat and holiday in the synagogue. It is really an expression of hope that one day everyone on earth will believe in the One God of all creation.

**HOW TO:** Just join together in prayer! Following the Nishmat Kol Chai, before the fourth cup, many families sing here, as well.

נִשְׁמַת כָּל־חַי תְּבָרֵךְ אֶת־שִׁמְךָ
יְיָ אֱלֹהֵינוּ. וְרוּחַ כָּל־בָּשָׂר
תְּפָאֵר וּתְרוֹמֵם זִכְרְךָ מַלְכֵּנוּ
תָּמִיד. מִן־הָעוֹלָם וְעַד־הָעוֹלָם
אַתָּה אֵל, וּמִבַּלְעָדֶיךָ אֵין לָנוּ
מֶלֶךְ גּוֹאֵל וּמוֹשִׁיעַ פּוֹדֶה
וּמַצִּיל וּמְפַרְנֵס וּמְרַחֵם בְּכָל־
עֵת צָרָה וְצוּקָה. אֵין לָנוּ מֶלֶךְ
אֶלָּא אָתָּה: אֱלֹהֵי הָרִאשׁוֹנִים
וְהָאַחֲרוֹנִים, אֱלוֹהַּ כָּל־בְּרִיּוֹת,
אֲדוֹן כָּל־תּוֹלָדוֹת הַמְהֻלָּל
בְּרֹב הַתִּשְׁבָּחוֹת הַמְנַהֵג
עוֹלָמוֹ בְּחֶסֶד וּבְרִיּוֹתָיו
בְּרַחֲמִים. וַיְיָ לֹא־יָנוּם וְלֹא
יִישָׁן. הַמְעוֹרֵר יְשֵׁנִים וְהַמֵּקִיץ
נִרְדָּמִים וְהַמֵּשִׂיחַ אִלְּמִים
וְהַמַּתִּיר אֲסוּרִים וְהַסּוֹמֵךְ
נוֹפְלִים וְהַזּוֹקֵף כְּפוּפִים וּלְךָ
לְבַדְּךָ אֲנַחְנוּ מוֹדִים:

Everything that lives praises You, Adonai our God. Everything that breathes seeks Your divine guidance. For all time, You are God. No one but You is able to rescue or redeem us, to save us and nurture us, to show us mercy in times of disaster. God of all times and all living things, You guide the world with divine kindness and compassion. You who do not sleep or rest, awake the sleeping, support those who are falling, free those who are in shackles, raise those hunched over, and provide speech for those who cannot talk. Only You do we recognize as God.

From Mitzrayim, You rescued us. From a life of slavery, You freed us. When we were hungry, You fed us and continued to sustain us. You saved us from death and protected us from disease. To this day, Your compassion continues to help us—You have never neglected us. Please God, never abandon us.

מִמִּצְרַיִם גְּאַלְתָּנוּ יְיָ אֱלֹהֵינוּ
וּמִבֵּית עֲבָדִים פְּדִיתָנוּ. בְּרָעָב
זַנְתָּנוּ וּבְשָׂבָע כִּלְכַּלְתָּנוּ מֵחֶרֶב
הִצַּלְתָּנוּ וּמִדֶּבֶר מִלַּטְתָּנוּ
וּמֵחֳלָיִם רָעִים וְנֶאֱמָנִים
דִּלִּיתָנוּ: עַד־הֵנָּה עֲזָרוּנוּ
רַחֲמֶיךָ, וְלֹא־עֲזָבוּנוּ חֲסָדֶיךָ.
וְאַל־תִּטְּשֵׁנוּ יְיָ אֱלֹהֵינוּ לָנֶצַח:

27

# נִרְצָה
## Nirtzah: Acceptance

**WHY:** Some scholars believe that it was the experience of the Exodus that actually made the Jews into a people. Now that we are at the end of the Seder, asking God to accept the gifts of thought and feeling we have offered, we conclude our last cup of wine with the final promise, "I will take you to be My people and I will be your God" (Exod. 6:7).

**HOW TO:** Raise your fourth cup of wine and drink it —still relaxing—after you have said both blessings.

# כּוֹס רְבִיעִית
## Kos R'vee-eet
## The Fourth Cup

הִנְנִי מוּכָן וּמְזֻמָּן לְקַיֵּם מִצְוַת כּוֹס רְבִיעִית

Heneni muchan u'mizuman. I am ready to fulfill the mitzvah of drinking the fourth cup of wine.

בָּרוּךְ אַתָּה יְיָ, אֱלֹהֵינוּ מֶלֶךְ הָעוֹלָם, בּוֹרֵא, פְּרִי הַגָּפֶן:

Praised are You, Adonai our God, Guide of the Universe, who creates fruit that grows on the vine.

**Ba-ruch a-tah A-do-nai, E-lo-hey-nu me-lech ha-o-lam, bo-rey p'-ri ha-ga-fen.**

בָּרוּךְ אַתָּה יְיָ, אֱלֹהֵינוּ מֶלֶךְ הָעוֹלָם, עַל־הַגֶּפֶן וְעַל־פְּרִי הַגֶּפֶן, וְעַל־תְּנוּבַת הַשָּׂדֶה, וְעַל־אֶרֶץ חֶמְדָּה טוֹבָה וּרְחָבָה, שֶׁרָצִיתָ וְהִנְחַלְתָּ לַאֲבוֹתֵינוּ, לֶאֱכוֹל מִפִּרְיָהּ וְלִשְׂבּוֹעַ מִטּוּבָהּ. רַחֵם נָא יְיָ

Praised are You, Adonai our God, Guide of the Universe, for the vine and its fruit. We thank You for all of earth's produce and the land on which it grows which You gave our ancestors. Adonai, our God, have mercy on Your holy city of Jerusalem, on Zion, wherever You dwell,

אֱלֹהֵינוּ עַל־יִשְׂרָאֵל עַמֶּךָ,
וְעַל־יְרוּשָׁלַיִם עִירֶךָ, וְעַל־צִיּוֹן
מִשְׁכַּן כְּבוֹדֶךָ, וְעַל־מִזְבְּחֶךָ
וְעַל־הֵיכָלֶךָ. וּבְנֵה יְרוּשָׁלַיִם
עִיר הַקֹּדֶשׁ בִּמְהֵרָה בְיָמֵינוּ
וְהַעֲלֵנוּ לְתוֹכָהּ וְשַׂמְּחֵנוּ
בְּבִנְיָנָהּ וְנֹאכַל מִפִּרְיָהּ, וְנִשְׂבַּע
מִטּוּבָהּ וּנְבָרֶכְךָ עָלֶיהָ בִּקְדֻשָּׁה
וּבְטָהֳרָה: וְשַׂמְּחֵנוּ בְּיוֹם חַג
הַמַּצּוֹת הַזֶּה, כִּי אַתָּה יְיָ טוֹב
וּמֵטִיב לַכֹּל: וְנוֹדֶה־לְּךָ עַל־
הָאָרֶץ וְעַל־פְּרִי הַגָּפֶן. בָּרוּךְ
אַתָּה יְיָ, עַל־הָאָרֶץ וְעַל־פְּרִי
הַגָּפֶן:

and on the ancient Temple. Build the holy city of Jerusalem quickly while we are all still alive so that we may celebrate its rebuilding, eat of its produce, and praise You. Give us all joy this Pesach. We thank you God for the goodness You give to all. We thank You for the land and the fruit which grows on the vine. Praised are You, Adonai our God, for the land and for the fruit which grows on the vine.

חֲסַל סִדּוּר פֶּסַח כְּהִלְכָתוֹ.
כְּכָל מִשְׁפָּטוֹ וְחֻקָּתוֹ. כַּאֲשֶׁר
זָכִינוּ לְסַדֵּר אוֹתוֹ, כֵּן נִזְכֶּה
לַעֲשׂוֹתוֹ. זָךְ שׁוֹכֵן מְעוֹנָה,
קוֹמֵם קְהַל עֲדַת מִי מָנָה.
בְּקָרוֹב נַהֵל, נִטְעֵי כַנָּה,
פְּדוּיִם לְצִיּוֹן בְּרִנָּה:

Our Seder is now complete, according to Jewish custom and law. Just as we have celebrated it this year, may we together celebrate it in years to come. With our people we have gone from Mitzrayim to Israel. As we have stood as witnesses to Your covenant, may You continue to redeem us in Zion as you have promised.

לְשָׁנָה הַבָּאָה בִּירוּשָׁלָיִם:

May we celebrate together as a free people next year in Jerusalem.

**L'-sha-nah ha-ba-ah bi-ru-sha-la-yim.**

Now that the Seder is over, you may want to revise how you felt about it and some of your thoughts for the future. Use your imagination and talk about these things.

1. My most important memory of this Seder will be ______.
2. My favorite part of this Seder was ________.
3. The funniest thing that happened at this Seder was ______.
4. For next year's Seder I hope ______.

# אַדִּיר הוּא

## Adir Hu: God Is Mighty

| | |
|---|---|
| Adir Hu, Adir Hu | אַדִּיר הוּא. אַדִּיר הוּא. |
| Yivneh veito b'karov | יִבְנֶה בֵיתוֹ בְּקָרוֹב. |
| Bimherah, bimherah | בִּמְהֵרָה בִּמְהֵרָה, |
| Biyamenu bikarov | בְּיָמֵינוּ בְּקָרוֹב. |
| El bene, El bene | אֵל בְּנֵה. אֵל בְּנֵה. |
| Bene veitcha bikarov | בְּנֵה בֵיתְךָ בְּקָרוֹב: |

Bachur Hu, Gadol Hu, Dagul Hu
בָּחוּר הוּא. גָּדוֹל הוּא. דָּגוּל הוּא.
Hadur Hu, Vatik Hu, Zakkai Hu,
הָדוּר הוּא. וָתִיק הוּא. זַכַּאי הוּא.
Chasid Hu, Tahor Hu, Yachid Hu,
חָסִיד הוּא. טָהוֹר הוּא. יָחִיד הוּא.
Kabir Hu, Lamud Hu, Melech Hu,
כַּבִּיר הוּא. לָמוּד הוּא. מֶלֶךְ הוּא.
Norah Hu, Sagiv Hu, Izzuz Hu
נוֹרָא הוּא. סַגִּיב הוּא. עִזּוּז הוּא.
Podeh Hu, Tzadik Hu, Kadosh Hu
פּוֹדֶה הוּא. צַדִּיק הוּא. קָדוֹשׁ הוּא.
Rachum Hu, Shaddai Hu, Takif Hu
רַחוּם הוּא. שַׁדַּי הוּא. תַּקִּיף הוּא.

# אֶחָד מִי יוֹדֵעַ?

## Echad Mi Yodeah: Who Knows One

Who knows one? I know one.
One is our God in heaven and on earth.

Who knows two? I know two.
Two are the tablets of the covenant.
One is our God in heaven and on earth.

Who knows three? I know three.
Three are the patriarchs.
Two are the tablets of the covenant.
One is our God in heaven and on earth.

Who knows four? I know four.
Four are the matriarchs.
Three are the patriarchs.
Two are the tablets of the covenant.
One is our God in heaven and on earth.

Who knows five? I know five.
Five are the books of the Torah.
Four are the matriarchs.
Three are the patriarchs.
Two are the tablets of the covenant.
One is our God in heaven and on earth.

Who knows six? I know six.
Six are the sections of the Mishnah.
Five are the books of the Torah.
Four are the matriarchs.
Three are the patriarchs.
Two are the tablets of the covenant.
One is our God in heaven and on earth.

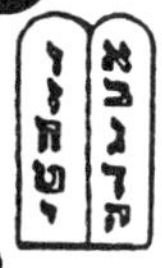

Who knows seven? I know seven.
Seven are the days of the week.
Six are the sections of the Mishnah.
Five are the books of the Torah.
Four are the matriarchs.
Three are the patriarchs.
Two are the tablets of the covenant.
One is our God in heaven and on earth.

Who knows eight? I know eight.
Eight are the days to circumcision.
Seven are the days of the week.
Six are the sections of the Mishnah.
Five are the books of the Torah.
Four are the matriarchs.
Three are the patriarchs.
Two are the tablets of the covenant.
One is our God in heaven and on earth.

Who knows nine? I know nine.
Nine are the months of childbirth.
Eight are the days to circumcision.
Seven are the days of the week.
Six are the sections of the Mishnah.
Five are the books of the Torah.
Four are the matriarchs.
Three are the patriarchs.
Two are the tablets of the covenant.
One is our God in heaven and on earth.

Who knows ten? I know ten.
Ten are the commandments from Sinai.
Nine are the months of childbirth.
Eight are the days to circumcision.
Seven are the days of the week.
Six are the sections of the Mishnah.
Five are the books of the Torah.
Four are the matriarchs.
Three are the patriarchs.
Two are the tablets of the covenant.
One is our God in heaven and on earth.

Who knows eleven? I know eleven.
Eleven are the stars in Joseph's dream.
Ten are the commandments from Sinai.
Nine are the months of childbirth.

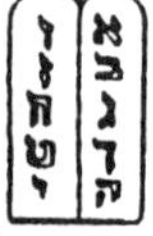

Eight are the days to circumcision.
Seven are the days of the week.
Six are the sections of the Mishnah.
Five are the books of the Torah.
Four are the matriarchs.
Three are the patriarchs.
Two are the tablets of the covenant.
One is our God in heaven and on earth.

Who knows twelve? I know twelve.
Twelve are the tribes of Israel.
Eleven are the stars in Joseph's dream.
Ten are the commandments from Sinai.
Nine are the months to childbirth.
Eight are the days to circumcision.
Seven are the days of the week.
Six are the sections of the Mishnah.
Five are the books of the Torah.
Four are the matriarchs.
Three are the patriarchs.
Two are the tablets of the covenant.
One is our God in heaven and on earth.

Who knows thirteen? I know thirteen.
Thirteen are the attributes of God.
Twelve are the tribes of Israel.
Eleven are the stars in Joseph's dream.
Ten are the commandments from Sinai.
Nine are the months of childbirth.
Eight are the days to circumcision.
Seven are the days of the week.
Six are the sections of the Mishnah.
Five are the books of the Torah.
Four are the matriarchs.
Three are the patriarchs.
Two are the tablets of the covenant.
One is our God in heaven and on earth.

Here is a game you will enjoy playing. The first two columns give the verses of "Echad Mi Yodeah" as they appear in the Haggadah. On the right-hand side, think of an original verse related to the number and share it with it the other members of your Seder.

| Who knows? | I know | I know |
|---|---|---|
| One | One is our God in heaven and earth. | |
| Two | Two are the tablets of the covenant. | |
| Three | Three are the patriarchs. | |
| Four | Four are the matriarchs. | |
| Five | Five are the books of the Torah. | |
| Six | Six are the sections of the Mishnah. | |
| Seven | Seven are the days of the week. | |
| Eight | Eight are the days to circumcision. | |
| Nine | Nine are the months to childbirth. | |
| Ten | Ten are Commandments from Sinai. | |
| Eleven | Eleven are the stars in Joseph's dream. | |
| Twelve | Twelve are the tribes of Israel. | |
| Thirteen | Thirteen are the attributes of God. | |

# חַד גַּדְיָא.

## Chad Gadya: Just One Kid

One kid, just one kid.
My father bought for two zuzim, one kid, just one kid.

Then came a cat and ate the kid
that my father bought for two zuzim.
Chad gadya, chad gadya.

Then came a dog and bit the cat
that ate the kid
that my father bought for two zuzim.
Chad gadya, chad gadya.

Then came a stick and beat the dog
that bit the cat that ate the kid
that my father bought for two zuzim.
Chad gadya, chad gadya.

Then came a fire and burnt the stick
that beat the dog that bit the cat that ate the kid
that my father bought for two zuzim.
Chad gadya, chad gadya.

Then came water and quenched the fire
that burnt the stick that beat the dog
that bit the cat that ate the kid
that my father bought for two zuzim.
Chad gadya, chad gadya.

Then came an ox and drank the water
that quenched the fire that burnt the stick
that beat the dog that bit the cat that ate the kid
that my father bought for two zuzim.
Chad gadya, chad gadya.

Then came a shochet and slaughtered the ox
that drank the water that quenched the fire
that burnt the stick that beat the dog
that bit the cat that ate the kid
that my father bought for two zuzim.
Chad gadya, chad gadya.

Then came the angel of
death who killed the
shochet
who slaughtered the ox that
drank the water
that quenched the fire that
burnt the stick
that beat the dog that bit the
cat that ate the kid
that my father bought for
two zuzim.
Chad gadya, chad gadya.

Then came the Holy One
and killed the angel of
death
who killed the shochet
who slaughtered the ox
that drank the water
that quenched the fire
that burnt the stick
that beat the dog
that bit the cat
that ate the kid
that my father bought for
two zuzim.
Chad gadya, chad gadya.

Take each character in the story in Chad Gadya, and as you sing the song and the character or object is about to be sung, create a sound for the character. For example, when the cat is mentioned, someone says a "meow". When the dog is mentioned someone says "bow wow," and so on.

Try to sing all of Chad Gadya in one breath, one verse per person, moving around the table with each succeeding verse.

Chad Gadya has been explained as a story describing Israel's trials with its enemies throughout history. Everything mentioned in the song is a symbol. The kid represents Israel, the father is God, the zuzim are the two tablets of the law, and the remaining figures are Israel's enemies: Assyria (the cat), Babylon (the dog), Persia (the stick), Greece (the fire), Rome (the water), the Saracens (the ox), the crusaders (the slaughterer), and the Ottoman Turks (the angel of death).

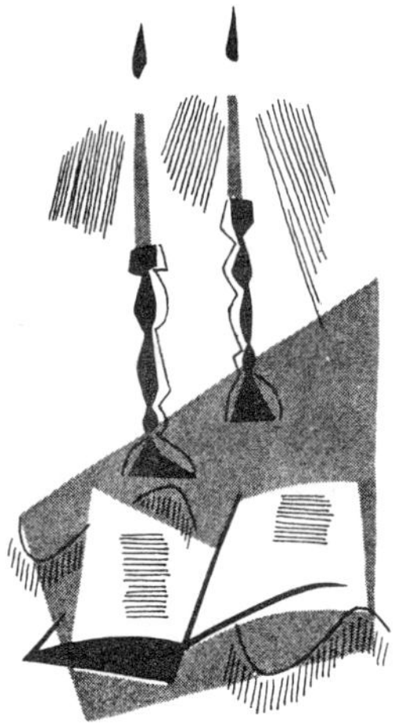

# כִּי לוֹ נָאֶה

## Ki Lo Nae'h: To You, Only to You

אַדִּיר בִּמְלוּכָה. בָּחוּר כַּהֲלָכָה. גְּדוּדָיו יֹאמְרוּ לוֹ.
Adir bim-luchah, bachur ka-halacha, gedudav yomru lo

*Refrain* לְךָ וּלְךָ. לְךָ כִּי לְךָ. לְךָ אַף לְךָ. לְךָ יְיָ הַמַּמְלָכָה.
כִּי לוֹ נָאֶה. כִּי לוֹ יָאֶה:
Lecha u'lecha, lecha ki lecha, lecha af lecha.
lecha adonai ha-mamlachah.
Ki lo na'eh, ki lo ya'eh

דָּגוּל בִּמְלוּכָה. הָדוּר כַּהֲלָכָה. וָתִיקָיו יֹאמְרוּ לוֹ.
Dagul bimlucha, hadur ka-halachah, vatikav yomru lo.
*Refrain*

זַכַּאי בִּמְלוּכָה. חָסִין כַּהֲלָכָה. טַפְסְרָיו יֹאמְרוּ לוֹ.
Zakai bimlucha, chasin ka-halachah, tafsirav yomru lo.
*Refrain*

יָחִיד בִּמְלוּכָה. כַּבִּיר כַּהֲלָכָה. לִמּוּדָיו יֹאמְרוּ לוֹ.
Yachid bimluchah, kabir ka-halachah limudav yomru lo.
*Refrain*

מוֹשֵׁל בִּמְלוּכָה. נוֹרָא כַּהֲלָכָה. סְבִיבָיו יֹאמְרוּ לוֹ.
Moshel bimluchah, nora ka-halachah, sevivav yomru lo.
*Refrain*

עָנָיו בִּמְלוּכָה. פּוֹדֶה כַּהֲלָכָה. צַדִּיקָיו יֹאמְרוּ לוֹ.
Anav bimluchah, podeh ka-halachah, tzadikav yomru lo.
*Refrain*

קָדוֹשׁ בִּמְלוּכָה. רַחוּם כַּהֲלָכָה. שִׁנְאַנָּיו יֹאמְרוּ לוֹ.
Kadosh bimlucha, rachum ka-halachah, shin-anav yomru lo.
*Refrain*

תַּקִּיף בִּמְלוּכָה. תּוֹמֵךְ כַּהֲלָכָה. תְּמִימָיו יֹאמְרוּ לוֹ.
Takif bimluchah, tomeich ka-halachah, temimav yomru lo.
*Refrain*